How To Influence People

Learn How to Speak and How to Act So People
Will Start Listening to You! Start Leading and
Be the Role Model Everyone Admires

Table of Contents

Introduction...4

Chapter 1: Are You Willing to Ask? 7

Chapter 2: 10 Foolproof Ways to Influence People............................13

Chapter 3: 15 Golden Rules for Mastering Small Talk.......................24

Chapter 4: 7 Essential Traits of Leaders and Role Models.................34

Chapter 5: 10 Infallible Steps to Increase Your Influence.................42

Chapter 6: Proven Tips to be a Charismatic Public Speaker.............48

Conclusion...53

Introduction

Ever wondered how some people can get others to do exactly what they want? Or how they garner a large following of folks who are more than eager to agree with them or follow their instructions? What are the secret life skills that these people use in the real world to influence people and get them to agree to things?

Mastering the fine art of winning and influencing people is an asset for life. It allows you to bring the best out of others, encourages them to see things from your perspective and ultimately helps them do exactly what you want them to.

It is important to understand that none of the techniques described in the book falls under the dark art strategies of persuading people. Influencing people isn't about destroying their self-esteem to feel great about self.

Au contraire, it is about building them up by encouraging and inspiring them. There are multiple psychological strategies to influence people without making them feel miserable about themselves. We take a hugely positive and constructive approach when it comes to being an amazing leader and influencing people in the right direction.

Wonder why some leaders inspire a following that goes all out to please them while others can barely get people to acknowledge their instructions? It is about building a connection that drives people in the right direction. Much as pop psychology writers wouldn't want you to believe this, influencing people is more than a bunch of psychological tricks. It runs deeper into people's emotions, their subconscious minds, and their most compelling motivators.

According to a legend doing the rounds, Benjamin Franklin had once wanted to please a man who didn't like him much. He went ahead and asked the man to lend him (Franklin) a rare publication. When Franklin received it, he went ahead and thanked the man graciously. The result – the two become great friends.

In Franklin's own words, "He that has once done kindness will be more ready to do you another than he whom you yourself have obliged." Seemingly small acts like (saying a thank you or being gracious) these go a long way in forging bonds where people truly like you and listen to you.

Have you heard of conversation hypnosis? The term has gained much momentum recently and is nothing but a series of techniques used for subconsciously influencing an individual or group's behavior in such as way that they believe their opinion has changed with their own will.

Of course, this area of persuading/ influencing people falls in the gray zone. Influencing people with them believing that it is through their volition can be misleading. It is for every individual to determine whether they want to use these tricks ethically or no. However, there are plenty of proven white-hat techniques to get you started with talking and behaving in a way that makes people sit up and take note.

Effective communication forms the basis of both – your personal and professional encounters. The words, actions, and gestures you use to connect with people help them understand you and make it easier for you to influence their actions in your favor.

Influencing people subtly is all about being a powerful communicator, charismatic leader, and persuasive individual. There are tons of ways through which you can get people to agree with you without being argumentative or negative. This book tells you how. It helps you understand how people react to different stimuli, what drives them to do what they do and how to encourage/inspire them in positive ways. Let's get started right away.

Chapter 1: Are You Willing to Ask?

We've been constantly fed on psychological theories on how just about anyone can become a leader. It is easy, right? A few leadership tricks up the sleeve and whoosh, you're an able leader. Nope. That's not the way it works in the real world. Genuine leaders are rare, simply because not everyone is willing to do the one huge thing they really need to for building their influence. Not everyone becomes a leader. But does everyone have it in them to become one? A resounding yes.

What is the one thing that the planet's best leaders know and the average folks don't? How do they connect with the world's movers and shakers, while spreading their wings? You'll notice that while some people are constantly growing from strength to strength (writing guests blogs, networking with the big players and growing their business), others are struggling to stay afloat. Even with all other things being the same. What is that one trait that separates winners from average mongers? Why do some people keep growing their influence over the years? This blatantly simple yet overlooked secret has been closely guarded by everyone from dynasties to politicians to salesmen to large corporations.

The answer is not really what you're prepared for – Ask. Stumped? Why do we overlook something so basic? You may not be a persuasive or charismatic leader (heck, most average folks aren't and if you are, hello John. F. Kennedy!) or even possess inherent communication skills for winning people. You may be struggling with confidence or self-esteem related issues. You may not have any special skills for wooing people (let's just assume there's nothing extraordinary about you).

However, you have that one special weapon, which though everyone else has, few use. This naturally gives you an edge over others who do not use it. The power to ask. Sometimes, you'll be surprised at what you'll receive when you simply ask. By not asking, your chances of getting what you want are 0%. However, by asking, there is at least a small percentage, a teeny-weeny chance of you getting what you want.

How many times have you written to the Queen of England or the Dalai Lama or other international/figures celebrities? None? Why? Owing to heavy doubt that these extremely busy figures will never make time to reply to an inconsequential individual like you. Yet, you'll be surprised to know how many living rooms across the world are adorned with letters from these seemingly elusive international figures. Why did some people get them while others didn't? Simply because the ones who got them increased their chances by asking.

Want a great worker to be a part of your team? Ask. Looking for a promotion or raise? Ask. Want to make a business decision keeping the interests of your employees? Ask.

A small act of asking can trigger a large chain of events and open up bountiful opportunities for you. You never know when one opportunity leads to another, and ultimately takes you places, while increasing your influence. Leaders and influential folks are not a result of a fluke. They know how to go out there and ask for exactly what they want or what they want others to do.

Sometimes even the biggest folks make themselves open and available to new ideas presented by seemingly "average Joes", so go out there and ask. You may want to create a social campaign or drive in your local area and may need volunteers or the support of your community. How do you get it? Ask.

Those bold enough to ask are often rewarded many times over simply because they dared to ask.

Asking is the difference between being a bestselling writer with copious royalty and a struggling writer whose manuscript is still collecting dust on shelves. When you ask, you boost your chances of making it happen, and create a series of favorable, fortunate conditions for yourself. As you can see for yourself – it isn't much about luck. It is about unlocking a treasure trove of good fortune and influence simply by asking. The new-age leadership is all about accessibility, and they are waiting to reach out to people who care to simply ask.

The number one trait that probably keeps us from succeeding or gaining influence is self-doubt. We have this lousy habit of not considering ourselves worthy or deserving enough of greatness. The belief that we "don't have what it takes to succeed" or fear of failure/sabotage ruins more lives than actual failure.

Sometimes we just make up our mind in a single, constricted direction, and no amount of persuasion works. In simple words, we are our most lethal enemy. How many times have you stopped yourself from mailing a person who can grow your influence simply because you thought that the person will be too busy to respond?

A while ago, I persuaded a cousin to email someone she has greatly admired over the years. She just wouldn't send that email because her mind was already made up. She had automatically assumed that this person was way too occupied to respond to an insignificant nobody like herself. I tried every trick in the book to convince her and ultimately got her to send the email. Bingo, the person responded almost immediately.

My cousin just couldn't believe what had happened. In her mind, she had already said "no" and shut herself from the prospect of getting a reply. Want to know a secret? Most people are accessible if we just believe that we are important enough for them to be glad to hear from us.

Want to connect with someone? Invite someone for coffee or dinner? Go on a date? Get someone's contact details? Get a meeting or appointment? Ask. The ultimate secret to winning a large following and influencing people is that just about anyone can achieve it. All you have to do is – ask.

Sometimes you have everything going for you in terms of skills, abilities and more, and yet you wonder why you aren't successful when it comes to influencing people or networking with powerful folks to grow your influence. Simple – you hesitated to ask. In your mind, you've already negated the prospect.

There's an easier way to get what you want or as they the old saying goes that the quickest route between two points is often a straight line. Though we come up with multiple convoluted plans and complicated strategies, the simplest way to get people to do what we want is to ask them.

Why are you wallowing in self-pity while your crush has gone out on a date with someone else? You feared rejected or coming across as stupid. And now the joke is on you, harsh as that sounds. Asking someone out or for what matter anything can be a scary prospect. However, isn't it better than simply waiting? Or letting a brilliant opportunity slip from right under your nose.

There's something irresistible about confident, self-assured and controlled folks that get them the desired attention. You bring the spotlight on you when you set aside all shreds of nervousness and ask. Be normal. Relax. Leave aside all nervousness. Be assertive yet polite while asking. More often than not, you'll get exactly what you want.

However, please don't consider asking as the magic diamond bullet for success. Sometimes, you'll have to be prepared to get no for an answer, which is alright since not asking is a downright no anyway. You may ask for leave, and not get it. You may ask for volunteers for a community drive and not get them. People may spend some time in consideration and refuse. That still pretty much comes close to not asking at all. At least, you'll have the satisfaction of trying. And you never know, you may be paving the way for future opportunities.

One of my actor friends auditioned for a role much against her wishes (she knew she wouldn't bag it and it would kill her spirit). As predicted by her, she didn't manage to snag the much coveted role. However, the auditioners kept her details on file and contacted her for another role (pivotal to the plot) a few months down the line. She bagged the role, performed wonderfully, and even went on to bag a few more productions post to launch a successful stint. If opportunity doesn't knock on your door, build more doors and move.

People who know exactly what they want are greater leaders and influencers. When you ask for something, make sure the request is specific. This makes it easier for the other person to establish intentions and give you exactly what you want. Your request comes across as limp when you are unsure about what you desire. Part of being a good asker is to be specific about what you want and show the other person about how badly you want it.

Another asking tip that may appear counterintuitive to the above tip is to be flexible when you ask. For instance, if you want a long leave, you've got to be prepared to resume at a different position, with a different set of responsibilities. People who are too rigid with their demands don't go a long way. You have to be prepared to accept or compromise on certain aspects to gain something else.

People genuinely want to help each other in general, so it's unusual for someone to run down a valid, thoughtful and polite request. Most people feel good when they make a difference in someone else's life. They were probably in your position a few years ago, and relate to your request. Keep this in mind, and you'll feel confident enough to take on the world. And this will be your first step towards bagging that coveted "yes".

Also, you may have quickly resorted to influencing people without trying to win them over or strike a friendship with them. People don't take too kindly to being used, you know. Try to forge connections and friendships with people by asking, before jumping in with your motives. Learn to listen more and talk less about yourself. It isn't always about you.

You may be a fabulous performer but in all probability, the lead role may have gone to the confident performer who dared to ask for it. Don't sabotage your own dreams and aspirations by not asking. Act now. Start asking.

Chapter 2: 10 Foolproof Ways to Influence People

So what are the perfectly healthy and little psychological tricks that you can use to influence people or build a large following? Here are some surprisingly effective and consistently proven tips for getting people to do exactly what you want them to.

1. Ask Big and Scale Back

In psychological jargon, this is also referred to as the "door in the face" technique. It starts off by making a ridiculously unreasonable request from someone (which they are guaranteed to reject). Later, you return and ask for something much more feasible and less ridiculous (what you were after in the first place).

It may sound insane, but the idea is to make the other person feel sorry about refusing your initial request (even though it was obviously ridiculous). The next time you come up with something more reasonable, the person will feel obliged to comply. This is like the payback for refusing your earlier request, and they feel more bound to help you than another person. Several companies and salespeople use this technique to sell to their customers.

2. Use a Person's Name or Appropriate Title

Dale Carnegie, author of the bestseller, *How to Win Friends and Influence People,* has explicitly stated the need to use someone's name to make yourself more likable for the other person. According to the public speaking legend, an individual's name is the most pleasant sound they can experience in any language, and this has a direct bearing on how they view people who are constantly addressing the with their name.

Our names are an inherent part of our existence, and hence hearing them repeatedly sort of authenticates our existence. This, in turn, helps us develop exceptionally positive feelings about people who validate our presence. To influence people, you can address them as what you want them to be, so they subconsciously start thinking about themselves as just that.

For instance, if you want to get closer to an acquaintance or strike up a friendship with them, start addressing them as "mate" or "buddy" each time you speak to them. Leaders and influencers know how to get people to do what they want simply by addressing people correctly.

Address your employees, followers, customers by their name as much as you can. It establishes a more personal foundation for your communication/connection. No one fancies being just another number or account. People appreciate the personal touch and human element involved in being addressed by their names, and invariably end up liking folks who constantly use their name.

Using a name, title or type of address can have power effects on the subconscious. The whole point is that if you pretend to be a particular person, you will end up being that person. It is a kind of self-manifesting prophecy. Similarly, when you want to influence others, address them as what you want them to be, so they start subconsciously thinking of themselves as just what you want them to be.

3. Mirroring

"Imitation is the best form of flattery." To make someone take to you instantly, be one of them or better just like them. Mirroring someone's words and behavior is a primordial instinct. It quickly makes people think that you are part of the "clan".

Have you seen how clever salesmen often repeat the words you do or imitate your gestures just to gently persuade you to buy from them? Or how leaders speak "the language of their people" just to win the trust/confidence of their followers. They are doing nothing but using the highly potent mirroring technique.

When you really want to influence people or get them to do what you want, closely observe their behavior, voice tone and pitch, mannerisms, body language and speech patterns. Then, use the same in your interactions with them to make yourself instantly likable. Works like magic!

Research has pointed to the direction that people who are mimicked are likelier to respond more positively to folks who mimic them. The way this works on a psychological level is that imitating someone's behavior pattern or words makes them feel a sense of validation. This positivity directly transmits to the person who validated them by mirroring their behavior. They come to associate people who mirror them as positive and likable. Doesn't your self-esteem and confidence automatically rise when someone emulates you? And you invariably end up liking people who look up to you.

Another potent tip along the same lines is to paraphrase what people say and repeat it, which is also termed as reflective listening. This shows the other person that you've been listening to them, which sort of validates everything they said.

Therapists and counselors generously use reflective listening (which is why people love to talk to them).

This technique can be applicable just about anywhere from your employees to your friends to your partner. When you listen to people intently, and rephrase what they said as a question just to confirm that you are on the same page, you're making them feel more comfortable about interacting with you. They are likelier to develop positive feelings for you and listen to you more keenly because you've already demonstrated that what they say is important to you.

4. Fake Confidence

Alright, so you dress up attractively, sport a sharply groomed appearance, carry the most stylish accessories, and still wonder why people don't listen to you, follow you or subscribe to your views.

Chances are, you are missing the most vital accessory – confidence. Yes, you have to slay the demon of low confidence if you really want to inspire the faith of others. The clothes, accessories, and grooming can only carry you up to a point.

One of the most fundamental principles of confidence is that you can totally fake it even when you don't feel it. It is all about your body language, voice, expressions, and gestures (which are fortunately in your control). You can pretend to be a highly confident persona even when you're feeling like a lemon from within.

Our body language invariably impacts our mental state and vice versa. When you act confident for a long time, you end up confusing the brain into believing that you are indeed a very confident person. The brain then automatically reprograms itself and directs the body to be confident, thinking it goofed up somewhere. So, what starts off as a pretentious act actually leads to you transforming into a more confident and self-assured individual.

5. Work Your Way Upwards

This is, in fact, the opposite of the "door in the face technique". Here, you start with a smaller request and start working your way up once someone has consented to a smaller request. Plenty of marketers use this technique to get their audience/customers to buy from them.

For instance, you start with a small request like enlisting people's support for preserving the environment. This is a relatively simple request, and it is tough for people to turn down something like that. Once people express their consent, it is easier to convince them for other related requests.

In the above example, if you have a bunch of people from the local community who've pledged to support the environment, it is way easier to influence them to shift to products (purchase products) that minimize risk caused to the environment. One golden rule – Don't barrage your potential customers or audience with one request after another. Leave a couple of days between making the two requests and you should most likely get what you want.

6. Point Out Mistakes Constructively

The surefire way to earning a large bank of haters is pointing people's mistakes to them in a manner that destroys their self-esteem. Point out people's errors in a positive, healthy and constructive manner if you really want them to like you or listen to you.

Stay humble, grounded and neutral in your correction technique. Your feedback will be more heard and valued when you do it in a more rational and less offensive manner. People are less likely to listen to you or act upon your suggestion if you take off on a never-ending and vengeful rant.

Make it clear to a person that you aren't targeting them but only helping them or saving them from further embarrassment. Try something along the lines of, "Hey Roger, I noticed a few errors in the way you created those formulas on Excel. It isn't a huge deal of course, but you can start working on the smaller ones and work your way up if that sounds good. You can watch me do it too."

This sounds more honorable and is more likely to be heard by the other person than, "you're an absolute dud with mathematical formulas on Excel", which only ends up targeting the individual personally and makes them more defensive rather than open to suggestions.

If it's a paper, performance or project you are reviewing, do it constructively by starting with all the great things about it. Gently point our areas where there is scope for further improvement without sounding harsh. "Hey Simone, you've done XYZ exceptionally well. However, I think you should go over ABC once again because I feel you can add some more bits there to make it more power-packed. This will make your paper even more awesome."

Stay miles away from criticizing people in a rude, patronizing, blunt, harsh and exasperated way. It is always advisable to keep away from correcting people in public. Keep it limited to the two of you, and the person will truly appreciate it while taking constructive steps in the right direction.

At times, it helps to save people's face even when you know they are wrong. This inspires them to bring about a positive change and makes you comes across as more likable.

For instance, if you made a huge mistake in your workplace, instead of pointing you out publicly, if your boss only makes a general mention (so as to ensure that it's not repeated) without naming you, won't you develop greater respect for him? What would he've named and shamed you publicly even when you know you goofed up big time? You would've hated him for life. While both reactions serve similar goals, the former is more constructive in bringing about the required change.

The other side of this, leaders who are quick and emphatic when it comes to admitting to their mistake make themselves instantly endearing to their followers. When you don't admit to your fault and try to make someone else the scapegoat or pass the buck elsewhere, it creates feelings of animosity and increases the hate quotient directed towards you. On the other hand, you earn huge reserves of respect, loyalty, and credibility when you own up to your fault. People admire honesty, which further inspires them to have faith in you.

7. Agree to Disagree

Opposing views do not mean you have to turn your home, office or social club into a battlefield. People who agree to disagree politely earn much more respect and influence as opposed to people who shove their views down other's throats and completely shut off to any view apart from theirs.

It is natural for people to hold different views. Not everyone is raised in the same circumstances or background as you. People come with a whole lot of different experiences, circumstances and life struggles, which tints their opinion or views on different subjects. Seek to understand where they are coming from rather than being fixated on the notion of "they are wrong and I am right."

Figure out what motivates them, appreciate their different beliefs (even if it doesn't match yours), and put across your views in a factual and respectful manner without tearing them apart. People who respect others' opinions increase their chances of being heard and understood. Others are less likely to get defensive and more eager to give your views a fair hearing if you appreciate their opinion and take a more neutral stand.

As Dale Carnegie famously stated, "The only way to win an argument is to avoid it." Arguments, however healthy you think they are, are roadblocks to communication. Arguments cause a breakdown in the communication pattern. It doesn't foster any genuine information flow, makes things increasingly awkward and creates an atmosphere replete with bad vibes. In the end, the topic doesn't even matter. Everyone forgets what the argument was about, and only remembers the acrimony it caused. So chuck it really or put across your view in a more compassionate manner.

You don't have to agree with everyone. However, showing a little empathy and compassion for other's views goes a long way in ensuring a healthy and open-minded debate, which ultimately helps grow your influence.

8. Appreciate and Compliment People Generously

This isn't a secret. Yet it is astounding how many people actually fail miserably when it comes to simple acts such as complimenting people. Why is it so tough to offer compliment people sincerely? Do you know someone who is a great mother or writer or manager? Why haven't you told them yet?

At a deeper, subconscious level, we all yearn for appreciation. When you appreciate people openly and regularly, they'll develop an instant liking for you. However, on the flip side, don't use this weapon to resort to flattery. People are smart and can quickly differentiate between sycophancy and fake flattery from genuine compliments.

To make the compliments sound sincere, pick specific aspects that you truly appreciate in the person. For instance, "the half man, half woman painting of yours totally nailed gender issues with a lot of sensitivity and depth of understanding" over "your paintings are truly amazing."

Giving specific, well-thought and heartfelt compliments is one of the best strategies for being the ultimate people magnet. Just keep it genuine. Dishonest flattery has the exact opposite consequence, and people are smart enough to know the difference.

9. Smile

Smiling is one of the fastest ways to get people to like you. With the amount of grumpy, scowling faces spotted on the street, little wonder that people who sport a smile become instantly likable. It is the most universally understood gesture of warmth and affability.

Humans instinctively relate gestures such as a smile, touch, hug etc to affability. It makes us feel that the person smiling at us genuinely likes us and is interested in us, which makes us like the person, and return their smile to create highly positive vibes.

Research has consistently pointed to the fact that smiling helps elevate our own mood since our mind feels the way our body acts and vice-versa. So the next time you want to go about influencing people or being a leader, who wields plenty of magnetism on his/her people, just smile generously. It will radiate your inner warmth, and make people take to you instantly.

10. Help Others Own the Idea

One of the most proven strategies for influencing others and getting them do to go your way is to help them think it is their idea, which will make them more acceptable and less critical about it. They will be more charged about accepting an idea that they own.

Use the reverse psychology technique by stating the opposite of what you intend to get them to do. For instance, if you want to convince someone to go hiking with you, saying something to the effect of, "I really didn't think there was any use asking you to accompany me on a hiking trip since you're not an adventure buff, are you? You're simply prying on what you think the person wouldn't do and feeding him/her with ideas.

Offer lots of hints, suggestions, and clues to help the other person draw their own conclusion, which pretty much makes the ideas theirs.

This is a sum of how things go in our personal relationships as well, right? When you need something from your partner, you simply drop clues hoping they will pick it up and give you what you need to surprise you. How about leaving a bunch of travel brochures all over the place and then subtly stating you need a break from all of it? The idea will, of course, be someone else's. Wink wink!

Chapter 3: 15 Golden Rules for Mastering Small Talk

Studies have it that when you meet a person for the first time, they judge you within the first 4 seconds of the interaction. Yes, that is correct. They decide whether they like you or not within 4 seconds of meeting you. Scary? How do you win people you've only just met? I've got a magic potion for that too – it's called small talk.

Though it may seem pointless, small talk is a brilliant ice breaker that pulls down elements of awkwardness and uneasiness between folks. It makes you come across as a friendly and likable individual, apart from helping you develop a sound rapport with people and create a stellar first impression. Small talk also lays the base for a rewarding and gratifying relationship ahead. It creates a more positive and beneficial atmosphere that can trigger larger conversations.

When it comes to breaking that initial awkward ice and setting the stage of a meaningful/fruitful relationship, few things work as miraculously as small talk. Whether it is a business networking meet or a dating club gathering, small talk goes a big way when it comes to influencing people, building relationships and being a charismatic leader.

Ever wondered how some people consistently manage to get people to buy their drinks at the bar or make friends in hordes wherever they go? Why do interactions with some people remain etched in our memory forever while we can barely recall others? The answer is well, small talk. Here are 15 rules for winning people using the power of small talk.

1. Stick to Safe Topics

When talking to people you've only just met, always stick to universal, harmless and non-toxic topics (especially folks from another culture, place, race, religion etc). Infallible small talk topics include weather, movies, world economy, breaking news, and food. A pro tip suggested by social psychologists is to base your conversation as much as possible on common grounds. Identify the common ground between you and the other person and stick to those subjects.

It is easy to gauge a person's comfort level about a particular topic through their body language (unless they read a ton of self-help books like you and have learned to fake it). If their reaction to a specific topic is positive and enthusiastic, keep at it. Always watch out for the non-verbal clues when bringing up a new small-talk subject.

2. Ask Open-Ended Questions

The golden rule for drawing people into a conversation or getting them to share more in your initial interactions is to ask more open-ended questions. Influencers and leaders understand the importance of asking gentle and genuine questions that reveal that they are truly interested in knowing more about the other person.

For example, if you've just learned that the person you are conversing with is part of a local NGO, ask open-ended questions related to it. What inspired them to be a part of the NGO? What are the drives that he/she has been a part of?

Learn to notice what people are truly passionate about, and create a conversation flow based on asking open-ended questions related to that topic to learn more about them. If someone's innately passionate about exploring different places and culture, ask about their latest vacation. Keep away from controversial and personal topics. The person will quickly take to you if you sound genuinely interested in knowing more about their interests.

3. Go Easy on the Humor

Sometimes people are so eager to make an impression by coming across as witty and humorous that they end up rubbing people the wrong way, especially folks whose tastes you know nothing about.

To avoid humor from backfiring, go easy on jibes, sarcastic remarks or tongue in cheek humor. It may seem funny to you, but the other person may not appreciate it. Even seemingly harmless comments convey the wrong impression about you. Intelligent/smart neutral jokes/comments are alright to a certain extent, but don't make it personal.

Avoid trying to appear too clever or familiar by poking fun at folks without understanding if they are capable of taking it in the correct spirit. Take time to know and understand people well without acting all familiar and extra-friendly.

4. Disagree Amicably

To avoid making your initial conversation controversial, express your disagreement without diplomacy. Instead of launching into an acrimonious attack or defensive name-calling (absolute no-no), try a more politically correct (yet genuine) approach.

Say something genuine and non-controversial like, "that's an interestingly different perspective really. I am now curious about that point of view. Can you explain further?" you are stating that the view doesn't match yours without setting the stage for World War 3.

5. Be an Exceptional Listener

It's no secret. In a world where everywhere wants to talk about themselves, good listeners are highly revered. It is easy to influence people when they are convinced that you are genuinely interested in what they have to say.

People erroneously believe that being a good communicator is all about possessing top-notch speaking skills. That's only one-half of it folks. The other probably more important half is listening.

Being a social skills ninja doesn't mean you talk nineteen to the dozen without giving others an opportunity to speak. Influencers know when you let others speak, and respond in positive/encouraging manner.

Show people you are earnestly interested in what they are talking through verbal and non-verbal clues. Acknowledge or paraphrase what they say so they know you are actually listening to them. Nod, express with your eyes, lean forward and keep your arms/legs unfolded (to show you are open to listening to them) to reveal your interest in what they are talking through non-verbal reactions.

Everyone loves affirmation signs that they are being eagerly listened to, which in turn encourages them to reciprocate when you speak. Exceptional influencers, role models, and leaders understand the power of developing great listening skills to make themselves more likable to their followers.

6. Reveal An Interesting Fact About Yourself

Okay, this doesn't mean you launch into a personal overdrive about who you are dating or that your bank account has just clocked a million dollars. However, a fun, harmless and interesting fact about yourself makes you instantly likable to people. They will be likelier to tune in to what you say when they realize you trust them enough to share things about yourself. Don't make it too personal for comfort though – that's the golden rule.

It can be something along the lines of your favorite author and why you love his/her work. Why you chose a particular vocation or major in college? Why you enjoyed traveling to a particular place and enjoyed its vibe/culture? It should be like an interesting teaser of yourself (why you love cupcakes or why you decided to call your dog by a particular name) without sounding personal, boastful or over the top.

7. Avoid Conversation Deadends

There will be those awkward conversation gaps which you may not succeed in filling. The best thing to do is such a scenario is look around you for clues to revive the conversation. It can be anything from a flyer to other people around you to details about the venue you're at. There are conversation clues almost everywhere that you can start building a stimulating and meaningful conversation on.

8. The Fine Question-Statement Balance

Maintain a fine balance between making statements and asking questions. A successful small talk brilliantly mixes questions and statements brilliantly to create more wholesome sharing.

Too many queries will make it seem like a one-way interrogation. While too many statements will make it look like the talk is centered only on you, which can be highly annoying for the other person.

Role models know how to balance the conversation so people listen. Pepper statements with thought questions, such as, "I am really into aerobics and Zumba, how do you spend your leisure hours?" or "I really enjoy watching that reality show though most people think is scripted, do you watch it?

You're sharing your views but you are also giving the other person an opportunity to share his/her opinion. This back and forth technique gives you a nice, well-rounded conversation.

9. Empathize With People

Empathizing with people is one of the most sure-fire ways of winning their trust and getting them to like you. Don't confuse empathy with sympathy. Empathy is not about feeling sorry for someone or making them feel pitiable about themselves. It is about placing yourself in someone else's shoes and trying to understand how they feel or the emotions they go through.

Saying things like, "I really understand why you feel the way you do" or "I truly understand how you feel about this topic" or "it must've been so tough for you but you've shown exemplary courage" goes a long way in building rapport with people. This sets the foundation for an equation based on empathy, comfort, and understanding, which is what leaders/role models need to inspire in their followers.

People are likelier to talk and share their feelings with you when they realize you understand where they are coming from. Just don't be dramatic and pretend to weep crocodile tears in a bid to show you really feel for the other person. That's totally undoing it.

10. Keep it Positive

When meeting people for the first time, always keep the conversation centered on positive subjects. Even when you feel that the other person is threading on a negative or controversial terrain, gently draw them back into a more positive conversation territory. Also, stick to subjects which most people in the group have decent knowledge of. You're obviously not going to find a lot of takers if you start talking about stock market dynamics in a meditation class or group.

Stay with topics which offer minimal scope for disagreement, conflicts, and controversies. Keep it balanced and simple for a successful starting point conversation.

11. Body Language Speaks Volumes

Body language or non-verbal clues can probably convey much more than words. Send the right body language signals to create a more favorable impression, and make yourself more likable.

Tiny gestures like smiling frequently, nodding enthusiastically, lightly brushing your arm against the other person, maintaining constant eye contact, giving out a firm handshake, maintaining an energetic/peppy tone and other similar signals can go a long way in establishing a more likable and influential persona. Remember – you don't get a second chance to make a first impression. Let every gesture count.

12. Do a Little Digging

A little background work goes a long creating a stunning first impression. Whether you are headed to a party or an important business networking event, keep a few topics ready after researching the group's predominant interest. For example, if you find out that the host or business associate/associates are heavily into spiritualism or traveling or cooking, research trending/buzzing topics in those niches to start an interesting conversation. This will help you fit into the group more effortlessly.

You'll be able to make the conversation livelier and draw people out of their awkwardness. Scan the day's newspapers for prominent headlines, go through book reviews, read up movie reviews and ratings or learn about the newest health trend doing the rounds of social media. These good to know topics resonate with most people and can help you appear well-informed and worldly-wise in front of a new audience.

If you know the names of people you will be meeting beforehand, you can track their social footprints across various social networks (just don't go about stalking them and making it obvious that you are checking out their profile every 2 minutes). It is easy to gauge people's interests, attitude and views through their social media profiles. This will give you a good indication about their likes and pet peeves, which can then be utilized for striking a meaningful conversation.

13. Build on Similarities

This is especially true while interacting with people from varied cultures and backgrounds. Find connecting bridges and build on it at every available opportunity. Find a common interest, favorite cuisine, a book you both particularly enjoyed reading or some other nice common ground.

Even if it something seemingly cheesy like wearing the same shirt/dress or shoes, always mention it to set a likeliness platform. Humans instantly take to people who are similar to them. When people realize your tastes or preferences are pretty much like them, they will be likelier to listen to you or look up to you.

14. Don't Overlook the Grooming

While you may be excellent conversationalist with flawless body language, few things can create a negative first impression like careless grooming. Even though this sounds basic, a lot of people consider it insignificant and focus on the "bigger things."

Never attend any social gathering without showering or styling your hair neatly. Maintain goof hygiene and grooming. Use a pleasant yet non-overpowering fragrance. Keep a few mints handy in your bag. Sport a neat hair style (that doesn't keep distracting you), keep your nails well-manicured and teeth - sparkly white.

Wear clean and ironed clothes. It is surprising how many lose out simply because they fail to pay heed to these elementary aspects. Clothes and grooming add to your persona even before you begin speaking. Chances are, if you turn up poorly groomed, people may not even give you a chance to speak to them. Disorganized and untidy looking folks seldom influence others or act as role models by creating a favorable first impression.

15. Ditch the Greeting Awkwardness

Greeting people when you are introduced to them for the first time can be naturally awkward, especially if they belong to a different culture or region. You may be stumped about the appropriate greeting. Some people aren't comfortable even with a slight peck on the cheek, while others may not appreciate a lingering handshake. In such a scenario, it is safe to wait for the other person to make the first move. If they don't, keep it universal – smile your pearliest white, say hi/hello and offer a brief yet firm handshake.

Chapter 4: 7 Essential Traits of Leaders and Role Models

Have you watched the Disney's, *Lion King*? If not, I suggest you do it immediately. If yes, watch it again. This time for the innumerable leadership lessons it holds. It brings to mind Simon Sinek's quote, "There are leaders and then there are those who lead."

For those who aren't familiar with the basic plot, Scar is the discontented brother of king Mufasa. In his sinister bid to become the king, Scar tries to kill Mufasa and his nephew (the heir) at once. During Scar's rule, everything is in shambles. There's barely any food, the fertile land turns barren and animals begin leaving the kingdom.

There are many vital lessons here when it comes to being a leader and influencer. Leadership is not having a bunch of followers who take orders from you. It is about inspiring, influencing and positively directing your tribe by leading from the front. Leadership is about using power constructively to bring about change and positivity.

Let's just share an amazing leadership story with you to whet your appetite for more to come. I particularly love this one leadership tale that exemplifies how a leader/influencer leads through example.

This is an anecdote about a leader known all around the world for his principles of truth and non-violence.

A mother came to seek Mahatma Gandhi's help in getting her young boy to stop his sugar addiction. She had tried everything in the book to get him to stop his habit of consuming excessive sugar and finally knocked on the door of The Mahatma. She embarked on a long, arduous and tiring journey in the scorching sun, only to be told by Gandhi to return after a few weeks.

The lady was shocked. She had negotiated a journey spanning several miles just to get Gandhi to ask her son to stop eating sugar only to be sent back. "I can't tell him now not to eat sugar. But return in a few weeks and then I'll talk to your son." The mother had no choice but to return home tired and dejected.

They returned after a fortnight. Gandhi welcomed them and made direct eye contact with the boy, while telling him, "Boy, you shouldn't eat sugar. It is bad for your health." The boy nodded and vowed not to eat sugar. The mother was now flabbergasted. She simply asked, "Why couldn't you tell him this a fortnight ago?"

Gandhi smiled gently and replied, "Two weeks ago I was eating plenty of sugar myself."

A leader/influencer/role model leads from the front through their example. It is easier to draw people's faith and get them to listen to you if you practice exactly what you preach.

Good leaders know what motivates people and how to inspire them. They are humble approachable and value teamwork. Here are some commonly researched traits that leaders and influencers possess.

1. Leaders are Learners

Leadership isn't the be-all and end-all of learning. If anything, good leaders know/recognize the value of leveraging by learning from different resources. They are constantly reading, watching industry related videos, learning from their team members and basically doing everything to stay on top of their game.

They learn not to show-off their knowledge but to be able to guide their team more efficiently. There is a never quenching thirst to stay to date with recent trends and industry-related news. They will never hesitate to ask questions or have conversations that help them acquire knowledge. Yes, good leaders are phenomenal learners, which help them become better teachers.

Simba's influence as a leader grew only when he demonstrated a willingness to learn from Mufasa, Rafiki (the wise old baboon) and Zazu, the bird. True leaders/ role models are perennially committed to the pursuit of learning, growth, exploration and discovery.

2. Leaders Care

"People really don't care how much you know unless they know how much you care." If you aren't a caring empathetic and compassionate leader, your other strengths matter little to people. You may be an exceptionally skilled and gifted individual. However, lack of compassion kills it for leaders.

Influencers and leaders will eventually have people turn on them if they are merely drunk with a zeal for power without possessing the right emotions towards their followers. In the Lion King too, the lions preferred to starve to death over serving Scar. They felt a deep sense of betrayal. Even the hyenas (who felt Scar was their ally) dumped him eventually. When his true colors were revealed, everyone turned against him.

You aren't a true leader if you show scant concern for people's or your organization's well-being. Good leaders are always high on empathy for their followers, and this naturally makes them more likely to be heard and admired by their followers.

3. Leadership is Not Power or Authority Based

Leadership is not about being high on the syndrome of power and position. You can't by default get people to obey you, follow your orders and generally bow down to you because you are their leader. A leader inspires faith and admiration, rather than expecting people to follow his commands blindly. If people merely fear you without looking up to you, there's something amiss in the leadership style.

If you are simply giddy with power and lack sensitivity or decision making skills (keeping the interests of your followers and organization in mind), you're far from being a true leader/influencer.

When Scar rises to the position of the king of Pride Rock, he expects everyone to follow his commands and obey him without question. However, his vanity, poor decision making and lack of positive influencing contribute to Scar's undoing. People rarely accept leaders who shoot orders or misuse their authoritative position. Followers accept leaders who inspire and win their trust.

It is as simple as, lousy leaders only accept power, where as good leaders accept the well-being of their people before power.

4. Good Leaders Motivate

There is a popular quote that comes to mind, "a true master isn't the one who creates thousands of followers but he who creates other masters." Good leaders are threatened by the prospect of losing their hold on power. They encourage other skilled, talented and able followers to become leaders by guiding and motivating them in the right direction.

Great influencers are seldom insecure about their position and often go out of the way to mentor their followers into being capable leaders. When you encourage others, they gain confidence and high self-respect. This is a reflection of your own confidence and high self-esteem. When you show respect for yourself and others, it is easy to earn the respect and admiration for those around you. What goes around truly comes around.

Even while criticizing or giving critical feedback good leaders motivate. They use a concept commonly known as "the feedback sandwich", which is nothing but cushioning the wee bit unflattering statement with a couple of positive statements in the beginning and end. For instance, instead of telling someone that they haven't been much focused off late, start with how much you value the professional relationship, and how the company misses XYZ's (employee name) focus. You can end with, "you really matter to the company so I really want to know, what's holding you back?" This is bringing the "not too nice things" to people's notice while still offering them hearty, genuine praise to prevent deflating their spirit. Leaders know how to balance critical evaluations with both - positive and negative feedback.

5. Good Leaders Reflect Integrity

Good leaders encourage their followers to act with honesty and integrity, following their own example. Integrity is on the basis of a powerful leadership. When what you say and do is in congruence with each other, it becomes easier to get people to listen to you. Honest, upright and truthful leaders always inspire the loyalty and faith of their people.

When you act with honesty, your followers respond with equal measures of integrity. You can't pull up others for their dishonest ways if you yourself are acting underhandedly. Positional leaders merely fill in a post for a particular time until it's time to be replaced by another leader. Transformational leaders, like the Lion King, rise to the occasion and seek to bring about a positive change in the lives of their followers through their own actions.

Influencers use their influence positively. They are aware of the fact that with great power also brings along a greater sense of integrity, responsibility, and accountability.

How do you want to be remembered as a leader? Someone who impacted people's lives positively through example? Or someone who turned his/her back on his/her true responsibilities as a leader? The choice is yours.

6. Leaders Have Vision

Scar had zero vision or goals for his followers. All he wanted was power. This was rather evident towards the end when food vanished from Pride Rock, and he was unwilling to make changes for helping his followers. The focus was entirely on his position as the king of the land. Such leaders have zero vision, and often point fingers at others or make others scapegoats for their mistakes.

This kind of leadership only harbors frustration and stress. A true influencer will have a strong vision about where his people or organization is headed. He will have clear goals, positive motives and well-planned action in place to meet his team's objectives. Effective leaders and influencers are willing to accept the responsibility for their actions when they backfire. They don't harbor selfish or vested goals at the cost of their followers' well-being.

Good leaders are aware of the duties and responsibilities that their position entails in the first place. They are aware of what is needed for them to do justice to the position they earned. Being a role model is all about leading from the front, armed with a clear vision.

7. Good Leaders are Positive and Creative

Rather than being disgruntled about things that can't be done, resourceful role models resort to creating opportunities and resolving problems creatively. They are always upbeat, energetic and positive, offering everything from sound relationship advice to tips for enhancing work productivity.

They exude infectious enthusiasm that inspires everyone in a positive direction.

Role models and influencers know to maintain a fine balance between productivity and fun. They keep the atmosphere around them positive. It is easier to earn the loyalty and devotion of team members (which in turn results in amazing results) if they work in good spirits. If your team works in an environment balanced with playfulness and efficiency, they are less likely to grumble about staying behind a few extra hours to complete an important report.

Good leaders and role models inspire devotion to the organization/brand. People are inspired to go beyond their call of duty if they feel good about themselves and the environment they work in.

Chapter 5: 10 Infallible Steps to Increase Your Influence

In his international bestseller *The 7 Habits of Highly Effective People,* author and motivational speaker Stephen R. Covey elaborated how truly effective folks, who are constantly engaged in expanding their influence, lead a life focused on bringing about a positive change within their circle of influence (areas that are within their control). They overlook things they have little power over (circle of concern) in favor of things they can proactively change. They divert their positive, magnifying and generously enlarging energy to increase their circle of influence. Here are some foolproof steps to increase your influence.

1. Practice Empathy

People who are able to recognize, feel and understand others' emotions can relate to their followers or others brilliantly. This makes them comes across as more compassionate and sensitive beings that are completely clued into the feelings of others. It is fairly easy to influence and lead people when you win their faith by relating to their feelings. However, keep in mind that there is a difference between using empathy to influence people and manipulate them. Stay miles away from manipulating emotion people trust you with.

2. Be Proactive

Influence cannot be grown by lying still. It happens only when you engage in the right activities, develop the right habits and surround yourself with the right people. Being proactive means going out there and forging new connections by constantly meeting new folks.

Proactive people don't wait for opportunity to knock on their door, they go out there and create multiple doors for themselves. They take courses, read books, sign up for newsletters/updates, and listen to podcasts/audio book. These are the real influencers and role models.

3. Accept Responsibility For Your Decisions

One of the most significant qualities of an influencer/role model is his/her ability to accept responsibility when things go awry and give credit wherever due. This trait alone makes a person/leader highly endearing to his followers. There's plenty of respect to be won when you are honest enough to admit you goofed up and accept responsibility for your actions rather trying to pass the buck on to someone else.

When you accept responsibility for your own and your team's actions, you quickly grow your influence by building others' trust in you.

4. Appreciate People

Gratitude is another huge influencer/leader/role model quality. Efficient leaders know the power of simple appreciation for channelizing people in the right direction. A simple gesture like thanking people, appreciating the effort they put into a project or publically praising their skills goes a long way in inspiring their loyalty towards you.

Always choose to recognize the work or efforts of others and focus on lifting them as glowing role models for others. Few things boost a person's morale than being presented as a sparkling example. This not just makes the person feel wonderful, but also helps you reinforce what's the right thing to do. Everyone wants to be appreciated and valued, and will, therefore, be motivated to do things as they should be done.

Another tip that can make you an endearing leader is the ability to help people save face in a potentially embarrassing or awkward situation. The person will feel indebted to you for life. They will feel a deep sense of gratitude that you helped them out of a tricky situation, which in turn inspires unwavering loyalty.

You can help deflect focus from the person's blunder. For instance, if someone says something they shouldn't have said erroneously or accidentally, quickly change the topic before anyone notices or pretend nothing huge happened.

As a leader, you are showing people that you care enough for them to cover up for small embarrassments or misdemeanors. However, don't let people take advantage of your niceness. Ensure that the person is assertively informed in private (if it's a potentially huge deal) that you won't show similar leniency if it is a habitual offense.

Coach and mentor people instead of humiliating them. If you spot a sincere effort to change, help them change. Work together on strategies that can help them achieve their goals.

5. Show Abundant Passion And Enthusiasm

Have the proverbial fire in your belly for whatever you do. This makes you an irresistible influencer. People can tell the difference when leaders/role models do something just for the heck of it and when they are truly operating with endless reserves of passion. Seeing you demonstrate the right amount of passion and commitment towards a project/cause lights others up too. This, in turn, grows your influence. It attracts others to work with you in your undying quest.

6. Stay Consistent

Consistency and commitment is a huge influence catalyst. It accelerates your influence in the positive direction by revealing how dependable your actions. People who are reliable, steadfast and dependable earn greater respect and obedience that people who constantly change their actions based on what suits them.

Keep your actions and words consistent. Stay consistent with the rules you make. Be consistent in your attitude, policies and leadership pattern. Above everything, stay consistent with your efforts for fulfilling your/the team's goals. People who don't give up are able to attract plenty of followers. Consistent folks are seen as reliable and are the preferred ones to be trusted with brand new projects, initiatives, and responsibilities.

7. Find Solutions

Solution providers are always more sought after than problem diggers. Your influencer invariably increases if you possess a solution-oriented mindset. People flock to leaders/role models who have a more solution-focused mindset and are capable of coming up with ingenious solutions to the most convoluted problems.

Folks who use lateral thinking, constructively problem-solving skills and path breaking solutions are often people magnets. They become instantly dependable and likable for their innovative thinking and positive approach.

8. Ask Questions

It's puzzling how little people value this one single trait that can make the quickly endearing towards others. So many people choose to ramble only about themselves and overlook the need to know more about others. Display natural curiosity in people to come across as an interesting conversationalist.

People misleadingly believe that reciting a witty anecdote or intelligent incident makes they come across as a stimulating conversationalist. Wrong. It is showing interest and curiosity in the other person (not bordering on excessive curiosity if you get what I mean, don't start an FBIish interrogation) that endears you to other people and gets them to listen to what you have to say.

Talking about yourself is not just boring, but plain rude and repulsive. In whichever social or business situation you are, asking questions is a foolproof way to get people to like you and influence them. "So, how's work?" "What are your plans for summer?" "Which was the last film you watched?" Appear genuinely interested in other folks to pique their interest in you. Be an awesome listener, and you're on your way to being a social rockstar.

9. Be Relaxed

Relaxed, rational headed and steady demeanors are likelier to achieve success influencing people than emotional, volatile and demanding approach. Being level headed and unperturbed can win you more followers than an irrationally dogmatic attitude.

People tend to listen to you more effectively when you speak slowly in a calm, relaxed and self-assured manner. Launch into an angry rant of name-calling, and you're sure to lose respect over a period of time. Influencers seldom display extreme emotional reactions. They exude natural self-assuredness that ultimately helps them to influencer others about their ideas.

If you truly want people to listen to you, avoid issuing orders. It makes you come across as grossly high-handed and disrespectful. On the other hand, when you demonstrate that you truly care for others' inputs, people are likelier to respond to your request. They will feel belittled and do the exact opposite of what you ask them to.

Instead, make polite and respectful requests. Use the word "please" wherever you can. Instead of ordering a person to go on an outdoor sales call for the day, you can say something like, "Isn't it a lovely day outside today? Wouldn't it be a good day to do your outdoor sales call? Slim chance the person will refuse. Request in a manner that people find tough to refuse.

Chapter 6: Proven Tips to be a Charismatic Public Speaker

If there's one thing that distinguishes leaders from average Joes, with everything else being the same (talent, knowledge, skills), it is the way leaders talk. Leader talk is no magic language. However, it is everyday language spoken effectively. Leaders know the secrets of impact communication, and hence are able to draw a larger audience. If you've spent some time studying leaders, you'll realize there's something that sets them apart from typical employees. They exude an aura of confidence, an undisputed magnetism and clarity in communicating their message. Their vocal presence is enough to inspire and encourage the crowds.

From Benjamin Franklin to Bill Clinton, good leaders are exceptional communicators who've mastered the fine art of influencing their audience through their voice and words.

They understand that their charisma lies in talking in a manner which inspires people to listen to them. So what's "leaderspeak," you ask? Here are some proven tips that can get you to talk the talk.

1. Ditch Those Verbal Clutches

People often make fabulous points when addressing a group of people, but ruin everything in an instant or lessen the impact/effectiveness of their points by including throwaway phrases that do not contribute towards making the message more power packed. For instance, people often end sentences with "and other things" "so on and so forth" and "you know things like that." These are nothing but lethargic linguistic slips that happen when you don't know how to end a sentence/argument with impact verbal posture.

These verbal crutches are most prominent when you take a pause while addressing a group or delivering a speech/presentation. The unintelligible sounds like "er", "um" and "aa" can be hugely awkward and ineffectual. So are gestures of lip-licking, dramatic hand movements, and constant coughing. These are all distracting or listeners, and seriously hit your credibility as a speaker. The primary issue is very few of us actually realize there's a problem in the first place.

One of the best ways to tackle this is to use a phone app and record yourself speaking on a random topic extemporaneously for a couple of minutes. Then, go back to the recording and note the number of times you've utilized verbal crutches. This simple technique will help you become less self-conscious while speaking.

A good narrative and effective language is comprised of using definitive words delivered with panache and humility. Refrain from using terms such as, "like" and "sort of." It isn't just weak and ineffectual but downright jarring for the audience.

2. Use Superlatives Sparingly

When you drop "awesome", "fantastic", "epic", "incredible" and the likes at every given instance, it starts to lose meaning. Over emphasis on superlatives washes its real meaning. Each time a leader or role model assigns extraordinariness to commonplace things; he/she contributes towards making them sound repetitive, which means the really exceptional does not stand out.

So each time you're tempted to say that someone's presentation was amazing or the project was "awesomely" handled, take a few minutes to reflect on your choice of adjectives instead. Speak about how the project was well-researched, comprehensive and full of rare data. Generic praises or descriptions don't go a long way in inspiring people or getting them to listen to you. "This is very detailed and articulate" can go longer than "good work" in uplifting people's spirits, while making you come across as an effective communicator.

3. Resist from Pulling Back

Resist from trying to equivocate when talking about crucial or tough topics. It is understandable that talking about not so pleasant things requires huge verbal and personal courage, however, there's no point in pulling your punches when important matters have to be conveyed to the team.

Resist the urge to use sluggish language since using clear, concise language will only boost your courage and help you connect/internalize what truly needs to be said, however unpleasant it may seem.

Use concrete and correct phrases to describe the situation. Clarify your stand if needed. As a leader, you're going to have to learn to call a spade a spade. Practice speaking in front of the mirror if you get the jitters before a big or important presentation or address. You'll notice your gestures, expressions, body language and basically know exactly how effective you appear to an audience to make the required changes.

4. Simplify the Narrative

Use the age-old narrative for structuring your speech – Introduction, Body, and Conclusion. The less complicated your narrative, the easier it is to comprehend. Know exactly what information to include and what to eliminate to keep it brief yet impactful. No one likes to hear someone go over the same ideas repetitively. Ultimately, the thought loses its impact.

As a thumb rule, avoid speaking about more than a slide per minute, and more than four points per slide. If there's more information to be covered while you're addressing a group, talk only about the highlights, while you distribute handouts to your audience. Always attempt to open and close the presentation with a similar slide to maintain uniformity and a good symmetry. Use graphics and videos to aid your narrative and tell a good story.

Also, pay close attention to your inflection during the narrative. Too many aspiring leaders and influencers inflect up towards the end of their sentence, producing a highly annoying sing-song effect that makes you sound ineffective and timid. Inflecting down makes you sound authoritative and certain, which is vital when it comes to influencing people.

The uptalk or rising inflection talk makes you come across as an individual who lacks discipline, confidence, and mindfulness. Stop right now if you're doing this.

Cliffhangers are another absolute no-no for a charismatic leader. Many presenters reach a brilliant crescendo in their talks only to kill it all by not knowing how to conclude clearly and resolutely. This is especially true if you are influencing people to buy from you. You need to include a definitive "call to action" or trigger people in the right direction by ending the pitch persuasively. End with the required impact and a leave a few seconds for the audience to digest your closing remarks or questions.

5. Overlook Verbal Lapses

How many times have you observed presenters awkwardly disrupting the momentum of a speech by apologizing for a lapse no one even noticed? It's alright to stumble over a few terms here and there while addressing an audience or group. Unless it's a huge blunder with important ramifications, there's no need to stop midway for apologizing. Keep going as if it wasn't a big deal.

A majority of the folks don't notice these slip-ups until you voluntarily mention it, which draws pointless attention to it and takes the focus away from your main message. It doesn't just disconcert you but also throws the audience off gear.

6. Create Memorable Audience Moments

Most speakers mistakenly believe that the presentation or talk revolves around them. Nothing can be far from the truth. To make your talk more impactful, make it about your audience. They are likelier to listen to you and get influenced when they realize it is centered on them.

Recognize or appreciate an audience member, maybe a stalwart who has been working tirelessly for the organization and is due to retire soon. Hail a significant recent accomplishment by an audience member. The more you draw your audience into the limelight by recognizing their efforts, the greater are your chances of increasing your own recognition powers.

Conclusion

Thank you for downloading the book, How To Influence People: Learn how to speak and how to act so people will start listening to you! Start leading and be the Role Model everyone admires.

I genuinely hope it was able to offer you lots of proven strategies, fool-proof techniques, and wisdom nuggets when it comes to growing your influence and being the ultimate role model. Whether you are seeking to be a leader or trying to widen your social network, these infallible resources will definitely give you an edge when it comes to influencing people and being a person everyone looks up to.

The next step is to apply all the brilliant hints and tips you've read here. We can possess all the knowledge in the world and yet stagnate if that knowledge is not applied. So start acting on being the people magnet that you truly desire to be. It's all right there – easy and effective.

Lastly, If you enjoyed this book and found it useful, please leave a review on Amazon

I would really appreciate that, your support really does make a difference and I read all the reviews personally so I can get your feedback and make this book even better.

Thanks again for your support!

Here's to being the fantastic leader, role-model, and influencer you were always meant to be!

www.ingramcontent.com/pod-product-compliance
Lightning Source LLC
Chambersburg PA
CBHW051251170526
45165CB00004B/1662